Into the Light...

for women experiencing the transformative nature of grief

Sharon Olson

Photography by Fred Stassen

Foreword by John Schneider, Ph.D.

Printed in the United States of America
by Bolger Publications/Creative Printing
3301 Como Avenue SE
Minneapolis, MN 55414-2809

Typography and Graphic Design: Laura Smalley Reisinger

Editorial Support: Kay Kruse-Stanton

For book order/reorder information contact:
Sharon Olson
Rt. 2 Box 75
Colfax,Wisconsin 54730

**Library of Congress Cataloging-in-Publication Data
No. 93-93738**

Olson, Sharon, 1946 -
    Into the Light/Sharon Olson; Foreward by John M. Schneider, Ph.D.
    ISBN 0-9638984-0-X

In memory of:

Elizabeth Layton
1909 - 1993
Grandmother, Artist and Activist

S.O.

and

Joseph S. Schumacher, Jr.
May 6, 1942 — February 18, 1993
ACS Class of '68
Always a good friend

F.S.

Table of Contents

*"What is meant by Light? — To gaze
with undimmed eyes on all darkness."*

Nikos Kazantzakis

Introduction

My very good friend once told me that "coincidence" is God's way of being anonymous. Then, perhaps it was no coincidence when Fred and Alayne Stassen invited me over for supper. While standing in the dining room my eyes were drawn to a black and white nude photograph on the wall. I stepped closer and instantly a connection clearly spoke to me. The essence of that photograph had poignantly captured and distilled a moment from my own past grief experience. If I had experienced the power of that one image perhaps other women would also. Subsequently, three voices came together to create this book.

The first voice is Fred Stassen's photographic perspective which combines art and skill in creating powerful images and moods. Nude photography is a delicate art. When done effectively, it invites the viewer to be more than an observer of beauty and sensuality. Rather, it provides a medium for expression of human experience. Fred's skill at using contrast, setting, and form invites us to identify with our own moments of vulnerability, emptiness, and strength.

Although Fred never intended to portray grief themes at the time he took the photographs used in this book, the nudes seem to convey that grief initially strips us of everything we hold dear. We have nothing left but our capacity for survival. Some individuals, however, do <u>more</u> than survive.

The second voice is drawing on my own grief experiences and those of people I have known to write the verse. My losses include divorce, my children growing up and leaving, parental illness, career shifts, and growing older. Professionally, I've shared the sorrow of many individuals and families through hospice nursing.

The final voice became evident as I thought about the photographs in the context of a grieving process. Grief has the potential to be a *transformative* process which fits with John Schneider's grief model. At critical points in our grief we are clothed in a stronger presence of being. Transformed, if you will, into a wiser and quite different individual than who we were.

A final thought. Grief is a common thread that connects us all together. Perhaps through the words and images in this book there will be opportunities to know that grief has the potential to be foe <u>and</u> friend — something viewed from a distance and felt from within.

Sharon Olson

Foreword

When we experience a significant loss, the protective veneer of our self-image can be stripped away. The anchors we have to our pasts aren't around anymore. We feel lost, the path before us shrouded in fog. Life as we have known it seems at an end. We are lonely, helpless, empty. We fear we've lost a vital part of ourselves — the beauty and innocence of our best self. Our lives feel denuded of protection, meaning and comfort. Sometimes we are ashamed of who we are and what we've become as a result of our losses. We want to hide — behind clothes, roles, images that distort or deflect the loss experience. By validating this emotional and spiritual vulnerability we become more open to the potential for grief to transform us.

In my view, grief takes on three quite different faces, each empowering the next. We first discover the full extent of our nakedness — what we have lost and how we struggle to cover and limit our awareness of that loss. Then we see what we have left or what we can restore that heals, warms, or protects us. Finally, with time and support, we find out what it takes to empower our selves; to carry on, to laugh and to grow.

What is Lost

The task of this first phase is to discover how extensive the loss is. How does it affect us? How many ways does it render us vulnerable, helpless, without protection against its relentless stare? We discover what we have lost, what isn't there now or what's no longer possible. We struggle to protect ourselves, to keep going, to gain respite. With time, these painful and often isolating discoveries give us an internal image and kinesthetic sense of just how extensive this loss is.

What Remains

The worst has already happened. With time, we accept the fullness of our losses and the limits we have in protecting our vulnerabilities. We find what we have left. When we've experienced the full extent of our loss and go on, the protective veil of healing begins. We find the sources of support and nurturance that helped us make it through the darkest and most vulnerable times. We look at ourselves and our experiences in a different light, seeing the blemishes and the beauty. We remember what we've lost and restore what we can.

What is Possible

When we take the steps to move on, we can discover life's potential. Living fully after significant losses means we bring together the resources of mind, body, and spirit; and act accordingly. We act in graceful harmony with ourselves and our values. We alter our long standing beliefs and myths. Shame no longer forces us to hide and conceal. We see potential, possibilities, the strength in who and how we are. We reform and re-explore; we risk, give up the comfortable and familiar in ways that are empowering.

We may not appear the same as we did at the start of our grief. We are trans-formed. "Transformation" means that significant changes in form have taken place — a moving across or beyond the old form to something inconceivable before the loss. We need to trust our capacity to grieve such transitions, those outward shells or covers. What is meaningful to us will remain. We alter only form, roles, and appearance. Our essential naked, wonderful self remains intact.

That which validates our own process becomes a part of us. There is nothing to hide. We don't need to give power to the images someone else has if we love and embrace our own image. We let go of shame as controlling us. We accept who we are and how we appear. With our internal clothing, we are empowered to move beyond limits and imperfections.

Into the Light is a visually and poetically compelling validation of the private and internal grief process of women. Like the nude photographs, grief is a process to be experienced from within, not viewed from outside. Sharon Olson encourages other women to see themselves as they are, disrobed of the temporary distractions of successes, relationships, failures or peak experiences. She entices the reader to integrate images of the beauty and the beast, to forgive imperfections and acknowledge humaness. *Into the Light* is a celebration of the feminine experience of wholeness with all its diversity, strength and empowerment.

John M. Schneider, Ph.D.

WHAT IS LOST

A time of reckoning.

A time to accede to limits.

A time of emptiness.

How much of our lives is over, never to be again?

A time to mourn.

A time of sadness.

Awareness of grief is joy's shadow. It measures the fullness of our attachments. During such times we know we will die someday. We observe ourselves without benefit of accomplishments, without the distraction of meaningful lives. Loneliness seems to have no limits, no end.

We struggle against this cruel reality, fight it, question its fairness. Does anyone care? Does anyone know?

One day at a time. Sometimes only a few minutes at a time.

Thinking of a future without what's been lost. Life is an effort.

J.M.S.

Helpless

Within me
the magnitude of this pain seems as
a giant boulder.

Through the Keyhole Mourning

See me here in this moment where I am
physically and emotionally vulnerable.

Who can comfort me?
Who can console this broken spirit?

From within echoes whisper

"no one."

I weep not for today
           but for all the yesterdays.

Pushing

Kicking

Screaming

Fighting

Hurting

others.

An ugly stranger has entered my house

Look closely   it's me.

Waltzing on the Precipice

My partner holds me tightly as we swirl and spin through this thought —
"It would be less painful if I were not here." *Swirling...Twirling...*

Alone, I stand in the kitchen chopping vegetables.
A frightening thought teases this rational mind. The knife point moves up
under the nipple of my left breast. *Swirling...Twirling...*

This could be over quickly if I choose to stop the dance.
Swirling...Twirling...

My grief knows all the fancy footwork.

Dead

I imagine my death sometimes.
Imagining and choosing.
Contrasts not unlike
           raindrops to a raging river.

WHAT REMAINS

Then, just when we reach the bottom for what seems the hundredth time, something shifts. It's not a conscious thing. It's something from deep within us.

We're reminded of our best self, perhaps — our belief in God, a spiritual connection.

There is a spark of life.

There's something to laugh about.

We're moved by the caring of a friend.

We're needed.

In spite of ourselves, we're curious — what will happen next?

In spite of it all, we'll make it. Without knowing it, we make a choice — to go on.

J.M.S.

lonely, loneliness, lone...

Alone.

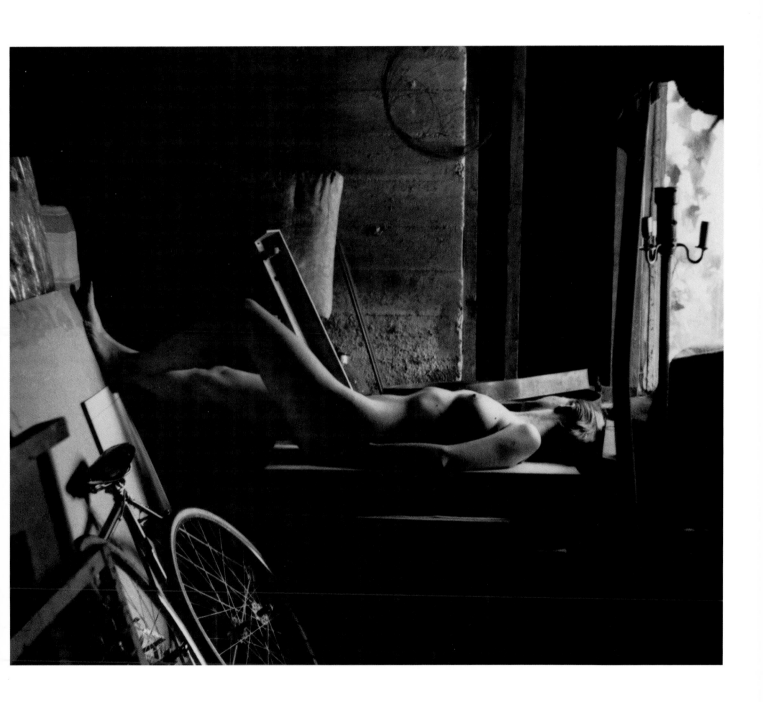

In Solitude

I conceive new perspectives

In Solitude

I birth new insights

In Solitude

I cradle my senses

Grief is there, in the shadows of our lives.
It is a solitary place which bathes us in the
half light of healing.

Some say,
            "Come out — come out and
                        into the light."

My soul murmurs,
            "In due time, friend . . .
                        in due time."

Washed Away

All that I *am*
        runs off my body and is lost forever.
All that I *will be*
        cannot be comprehended.

out

and

up

Rising   takes courage.

The butterfly risks.

Wisdom

No one can take my journey.
I must go *myself*.

We are bringing under one roof the paradoxes inherent in who we are and in what we've lost. We own parts of ourselves we have despised or denied. Growth means giving up protection, the kind afforded by avoiding conflict or choice, by denying reality, by staying too long as a survivor or a victim. It means challenging and sometimes relinquishing beliefs, assumptions and roles — questioning our basic values. When we integrate our losses, we relinquish the comfort of our sadness, the support for our loss, the power of being rightfully indignant. We move on — to an unknown future that lacks the familiar focus and predictability that living in our loss afforded us.

Finding what's possible involves empowering our fantasies in ways that turn some possibilities into probabilities, some dreams into realities. All we have to do is accept the outcomes — that sometimes the dream won't become a reality, that taking chances doesn't always pay off. If we've learned anything from processing our losses to this point, it's that we can grieve when we relinquish imposing our will. Grieving, as distressing as it can be, gives us the autonomy to empower the choices we eventually make, for we know we can choose and lose critical parts of our lives and still go on. Self-empowerment emerges when we realize we do have choices — real choices about living how much and how fully. We live the interlude.

J.M.S.

WHAT IS POSSIBLE

Forgiveness:
warm light in the cocoon unfolding

No further, no further with this grief!
It has pushed me so far against
the wall of life
that I can go no deeper.

WAIT! What is this?

Something within me starts to

                       push
                back.

Revelations

Finding *me*

Being *me*

Loving *me*

For the first time —

                again.

Strength to face a new day —
easy for some
major surgery for others.

Simple Truths

Two seedlings started as neighbors sharing the sun and the rain. One, a pine, quickly grew thin and tall spreading its roots wide and shallow. The other, an oak, grew more slowly with roots deep and branches tortuous from hard living.

One day the pine said to the oak "Hurry and catch up, my friend. You are much too slow." The oak just looked on and said nothing. That evening a storm came over the land, unlike any the pine and oak had seen before. All night it raged with thunder, lightning and torrents of rain. In the morning as the sun brought its first rays of a new day, one tree lay toppled while the other seemed...taller.

Moments of Wholeness

The sound of my laugh —
grief's soul scars stretching.

It amazes me —

      feeling joy,
          loving,
              living again.

Different

Stronger

Empowered

Grief — my spirit healer on this journey home.

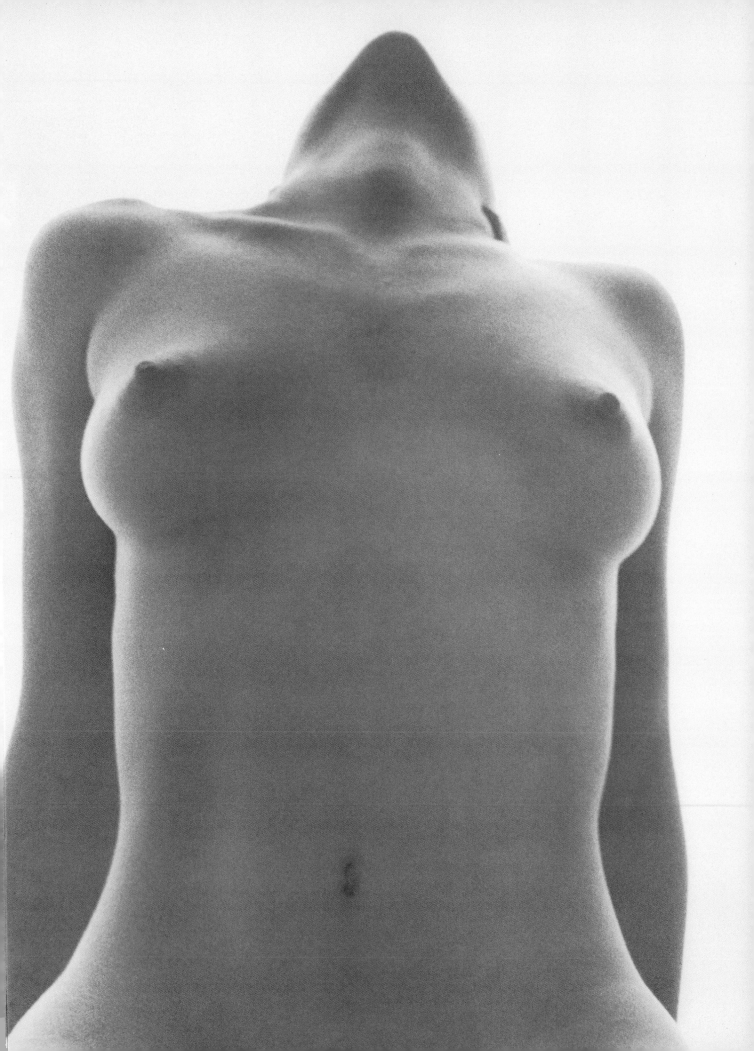

Sharon Olson Ph.D.

Author of
**Into the Light:
For Women
Experiencing the
Transformative
Nature of Grief**

Sharon is an Associate Professor at the University of Wisconsin-Stout in Menomonie and teaches in the area of family health issues, life span development, death education/ counseling, hospice and family caregiving. She enjoys blending music, creative writing, story-telling and other expressive arts to facilitate a better understanding of the transformative nature of grief.

Through various program formats, women have opportunities to respond to their own loss issues using:

- *Music and Imagery*
- *Story-telling*
- *Photographic response writing*
- *Creative Movement*

For further information please contact:
Sharon Olson
Rt. 2 Box 75 Sundown Trail
Colfax, WI 54730
(715) 235-1724

Additional information will also be provided on request for women's/men's/couples weekend workshop/ retreats focusing on transformative grief, conducted by John Schneider, Ph.D. and Sharon Olson.